INVESTING (ROADMAP) FOR SECURE RETIREMENT

DR RISHI SAXENA,M.D.

Dr Rishi Saxena is practicing cardiologist who has done investing in Stocks,mutual funds,Options,Bond market and Real estate market for 23 years. He has accomplished secured retirement using these vehicles to attain goal. He want to pass on factual information as part of legacy educating people what works and what does not work with real life experience of working in trenches to accomplish goal for over two decades. Hopefully this will accomplish goal or serve as roadmap to secure retirement.

Thank you.

Chapter 1: INTRODUCTION

Intention of writing this book is to simplify investing principle to a common person. There are lot of books available on investing but they either cover stock market or bond market or real estate investing. This book covers all, most important investing choices and written with clear no-nonsense approach to wise investing which could be read in 1-2 hours. I have invested in all these arena for more than 20 years and learned by own and other peoples mistake to give you concise no nonsense investing guide for successful retirement.

Life could be divided into 3 phases. First phase is Education Phase which lasts 25-30 years, where we educate ourselves to be a productive person in the society. The second phase is Accumulation phase which stretches out for 35-40 years (Age25/30---65 years) in which we continue to educate ourselves but trade our time for money to monetize what we have learned in first phase. In the third phase called Enjoyment and Legacy phase (Age 65 onwards), money works for us, so that we could enjoy life to it's fullest and fulfil our legacy.

FIRST PHASE (EDUCATION PHASE)

Priorities during first phase (Education Phase) includes try to find out what you like and what special skill God has given you so you enhance that skill by further education and training. Investing in yourself by educating best you can be. If you want to be Doctor.Engineer,Scientist Attorney etc, you need to pursue college education and advanced degree, with least cost and loan, and if possible working part-time during education to minimize debt. If college education does'nt interest you then you ought to pursue technical education after high school like Auto,HVAC,plumbing,computer technicians etc. to learn skill which could support you during later phases of life. If you want to be teacher,be expert in your field through education and training. Try to be the best you can be, based on your education,skill and interest. Next priority is to select right life partner to fulfill and support your lifelong dreams. I think this is the most important decision of our lifetime and could fulfil our dream in future or ruin our life.

Most of us end up with a loan at the end of first phase because of education and we're not fortunate enough for our parents to pay for college/ technical education. Part time work could help minimize the loan and financial burden.

SECOND PHASE (ACCUMULATION PHASE)

Most important things which we need to do in the beginning of second phase once we get job and get married is to protect us from any disaster. Steps to take to help us from disaster include:

1. Buy term life insurance 15 time your salary (Or Yearly need) so if you lose life because of sickness / accident, your wife and children are taken care off.
2. Buy long term individual disability insurance at least 80% of your monthly salary or need so in case you have accident/sickness, you and your family are taken care off.
3. Have emergency fund equal to 6—12 month salary, to deal with any disaster or if you lose your job.

During the initial part of second phase, 25/30--65 years, we have a lot of liabilities and the aim is to pay debts, smallest to largest which could include educational loan, car loan, credit card loan and arranging for down payment of house.

Once above liabilities are dealt with,

1. It will be wise to contribute to 401K particularly if matched by the employer.

2. Contribute maximum to Roth IRA ($6000 per year up to age 50 and subsequently $7000/year. For people who are not familiar with Roth IRA.This was started by Senator William Roth ,so Americans could put after tax money for retirement and it grows tax free during lifetime and money can be withdrawn during retirement after age 591/2, anytime without mandatory withdrawal. Contributed money could be withdrawn after 5 year of contribution

3. Contribute additional principal payments to mortgage loan based on savings. (Mortgage should be preferably fixed 10-15 years loan)

4. Contribute to children upcoming college education if possible via 529 plan. 529 plan is like Roth IRA for education and money grow tax free if used for education by children and is transferable from one child to other child.You can contribute upto $14000/year or $70000 for 5 years.

4

5. If you have high deductible insurance, you can invest pre tax dollars around $7000 for family in 2019 in Health saving Account and half if you are single and additional $1000 if you are older than 55 tax free and can utilize this money for your health care need in future .

.

By the time above liabilities are met with, and above contributions are made, we are about 45-50 years old. By then, we have paid a decent amount of money in children's educational account (preferably 529 plan, where money is growing tax free). House is preferable paid off or is in last few years of payment (<5 years) and, at this stage ,at age 50-55-year, primary aim is to go all out for investing for retirement. At this stage, aim is to contribute at least 15% of salary for retirement but put all the money left at end of month after all necessary expenditures are met with in retirement fund.

THIRD PHASE: ENJOYMENT AND LEGACY PHASE

Aim during third phase is to have financial freedom, so our money work for us, so we can enjoy retirement and leave legacy for family and other human beings so we are remembered for our generosity and deeds. We work for pleasure or pleasure and money not just for money only.

How to invest money for retirement

Basic principle of investing is buy low and sell high and choices for investing include Equity (stock market), fixed income (Bond market) and Real estate investing directly in residential or commercial real estate or indirectly via stock market by investing in REITs (Real estate investment trust)

Initially I will give details of how to pick investment in each category (stock or bond or Real estate) and subsequently how to allocate your percentage of assets in various categories.

Chapter 2 : Stocks

Stock or Equity

Stocks are pieces of ownership of individual or group of companies. Investing in individual stock is very risky and you may lose significant portion of your wealth investing in one or few companies. Example of single stocks which were famous in past but have disappeared or lost lot of wealth include household names like MCI-WorldCom, Toys'rus, Radioshack, Enron and companies like Sears-Kmart, JC Penny are on life support. On otherside you do not know which company will be next Microsoft, Google, Amazon or Facebook. Picking successful company for long term is like knowing lottery number in advance of draw which is almost impossible.

So my suggestion is to buy whole stock market all around globe through total world stock index fund since you do not know which company or country will do good over time. One year US market may do good next year Europe or Japan may do better and third year emerging market or Australian market may do better. Since you do not know future, it is good to make bet over global economy and have global diversification to minimize risk of future loss.

Here are ways to reduce risk in stock investing :

- Pick whole stock market as investment rather than individual stocks/sector.

- On average by investing in total stock market by index fund you are beating 90% of actively managed stock funds.

- Index fund carry low expense ratio (About less than 0.20%) so most of your money is working for yourself rather than enriching pocket of brokerage companies.

- With investing in index fund, you are minimizing portfolio turnover (Less buying and selling) thus amount of taxes you pay in non-retirement account is minimized.

- Ideal vehicle to invest will be index mutual fund/ETF bought from low cost company like Vanguard. By investing in Vanguard total world stock index mutual fund (VTWSX) or VT(ETF) you are investing in thousands of companies (Around 8202 stocks around the globe) with expense ratio of less than 0.1%.

This Mutual fund or ETF will cover most of the stock market and will keep it simple. Above Mutual fund or ETF will serve need of majority of people and will keep it simple.

Since above fund / ETF invest around 80% in large cap companies around the globe, You could further diversify by investing 70% of Funds in Vanguard Total world stock index mutual fund (VTWSX) or ETF VT and 30% of funds into Vanguard small cap index fund (NASEX), expense ratio 0.17% or ETF VB or I share ETF IJR (Expense ratio less than 0.1% . Fidelity has recently come out with Zero expense domestic and international index fund but these fund are brand new and I want to see composition and performance of these funds before recommending it.

Stock market is risky investment and your proportion of investing in stock market after age 50 should not exceed more than 75%, to maintain stability in your portfolio.

I do not want to bother you with too much complexity beyond it, but some simple facts will help you to become confident investor.

Future returns of stock market is determined by price you pay for earning (PE ratio) and Earning growth. Historically price earning ratio for stock market have been around 15 times earnings for several decades. But recently PE ratio for global stock index funds has touched around 20 times earnings, because of low interest rate and central banks buying of treasury bonds across the globe, first in USA followed by Europe and then Japan by quantitative easing. Future return of stock market may be negatively affected by higher price earning (PE) ratio. (Current PE ratio of 20 Vs historical normal of 15 time earning)

Based on above observation I will recommend that you reduce your allocation to stock market to 40-50% if you are within 5 years of retirement or in retirement already.

Next, we will deal with fixed income or Bonds

Chapter 3: Bonds

BONDS

Bonds are IOU (Debt) of any entity which include US government, Governmental agencies like Freddie mac and Fannie Mae., States, Cities, Counties, Towns, Hospitals, Stadium, Utilities and various Corporations.

Based on lending companies these bonds are called Treasury, Municipal or Corporate bonds. There are three major companies, S & P, Moody and Fitch which rate these companies based on their financial strength and ability to repay their debt. These bonds are rated AAA (Excellent rating) to C (junk rating) / D(Already in default).

Purpose of investing in bonds is to give, stability to your portfolio and give you stable income in retirement so there is no point investing in companies with junk rating. My preference is to invest in AAA and AA rated companies.

To simplify investing in bonds there are 3 types of Bonds.

Treasury Bonds

- These bonds are secured by printing power of money by government but gives you the lowest return. Return of these bonds are not subjected to taxation by state government but you must pay federal taxes on it.

- Currently yield on 2 year treasury bond is around 1.5 %,10 years treasury bond is around 1.5 % and 30 year Treasury bond is around 2%.

- Bonds which are issued by the government agencies have slightly higher return than treasuries but have slightly more risk.

- TIPS (Treasury Inflation Protected Securities) are bond issued by US treasury and their principal rises with inflation and could be good bonds to have when inflation is rising.

Municipal Bonds

Municipal bonds are debt obligations of States, Counties, Cities or obligation of specific projects like essential services like water, electricity or specific project like hospital, stadium etc. Most of municipal bonds interest income is federal tax free and if they are issued by your own state could be double tax free both by federal government and state government.

Municipal bonds are of two types.

1. Revenue bonds :

They are dependent on revenue from specific project like stadium, hospital or revenue derived from utilities like Electricity or Water services and also could be backed by toll. Revenue Bonds are more riskier than second type of bond called general obligation bonds .Among revenue bonds hospital and stadium bonds are riskier than essential services bonds like electricity and water services.

2. General Obligation Bonds:

General obligations bonds are backed up by taxing power of town, counties, cities or states. Mostly State general obligations are less risky than general obligations bonds of smaller town, county and cities. General obligation bond of financially sound states like Tennessee, Florida and Utah are less risky than financially poor states like Illinois and Connecticut.

Overall General obligations bond have less risk than revenue bonds.

Corporate Bonds.

Third types of bonds are issued by various corporations and offer higher return (yield in comparison to Treasury bond). These bonds are rated by credit rating agencies (S&P, Fitch and Moody) from AAA (excellence) to C (Junk Bond). Lower rated bond have higher return / higher risk than highly rated bond.

I recommend that people with tax rate > 22% should preferably invest in municipal bond and people in low tax bracket (<22%) should consider buying taxable bonds. Ideal way to buy taxable bond like stock market should be Total bond market index mutual fund (VBTLX) or Total index bond ETF (BND) with low expense ratio with company like Vanguard. Currently this bond fund / ETF have more than 8000 bonds Including government, agency and corporate bonds with expense ratio of 0.05%

Since purpose of bond income is for safe income in retirement. In case of individual Muni bonds, I personally recommend buying AAA /AA rated muni bonds from financially sound state and diversify over 10- 20 states. These individual muni bonds could be bought directly from companies like Vanguard, Fidelity and Charles Schwab. If you have small capital (Less than half million), you could buy municipal bond fund with low expense ratio from Vanguard (VTEAX) for the purpose of diversification to minimize default risk. This fund has over 4000 tax exempt bonds and have expense ratio of 0.09%

If you do not like real estate investment, then you should invest around 40-50% of your portfolio in taxable bond fund or municipal bonds (funds) to derive safety income particularly if you are close to retirement or in retirement.

Aim is to cover your essential needs from income from muni-bond or taxable bond funds, so that you do not get nervous with major downturn in stock market in retirement. This is like providing sleep insurance.

Purpose of stock market is to deal with inflation in retirement.
Next we are going to discuss real estate as investment and source of income during retirement.

Chapter 4: Real Estate

Real Estate

Real estate investment is hybrid of stock & bond investment. It gives you appreciation like stock market over years while giving you bond like return in term of rental payments.

Real estate investment choices includes investing in single family home, duplexes, apartments, commercial buildings including office buildings, retail stores, malls, industrial buildings, parking lots etc..

To start out it is good to start with single family home or small commercial building and gradually increase the number of homes and commercial buildings. Please make sure building is in good condition, reasonably priced and do not hesitate to get rental home or building checked by a inspector.

Please also get numbers checked by professional accountant that numbers make sense and you are getting good return on your investment (Cap rate). Good location is key for future rental and all possible tenant need to be checked for past record before contractual agreement is signed. If you do not have time to manage building it is important to hire a good professional management company.

When you are young you can use residential real estate to start out but as your number of properties grow you can start buying commercial real estate properties. Use lot of time to buy right property. Do not delegate it to somebody else.

If you have large capital you could consider using small portion of investment in buying properties with NNN lease (Where renter pays property tax, property insurance and all maintenance cost) to large corporation like Walgreens, CVS, Bank of America etc.

If you do not have time and patience to buy and rent buildings then you can invest in real estate by buying REITS (Real estate investment trust). My personal preference will be to buy broadly diversified, low expense ratio REIT from Vanguard (VNQ) .

Advantage of real estate investment includes:

1. Appreciation of value overtime.

2. Rental income helps you to get bond like return.

3. You could depreciate residential real estate over 27.5 years & commercial real estate over 39 years & that help to offset current taxes & help you convert current income to long term capital gain taxes / recapture of depreciation which has lower income tax rate than ordinary income tax rate.

4. You could exchange current appreciation of property price to buy different property via 1031 exchanges without having to pay capital gain taxes.

5. Over time rent could be increased based on demand for that building.

6. With current tax law, you could write off 20% of REITS income.

Disadvantages of rental real estate include:

1. Quite often it is a job rather than passive investment. It takes time to manage residential or commercial real estate to take care of plumbing, HVAC, roof leaks etc., . You could hire a management company to do job but that will cut your return and condition of rental is dependent on mercy of tenant.

2. Building, Roof, HVAC, plumbing, electrical fixture tend to deteriorate with time & will need additional capital to maintain rental in good condition.

3. Escalating property taxes, property insurance and liabilities will take away portion of your profit on yearly basis.

4. Especially in commercial building try to lure new tenant may involve additional capital for tenant improvement allowance.

5. Vacancies will keep profit down.

Investment in land is purely speculative investment with yearly cost of property taxes and upkeep & should be avoided unless you are insider knowing which side of town is getting new school or road construction or business.

Above information is based on my real estate investing in residential and commercial buildings over 20 years.

Chapter 5 : Option

Investing in option is very risky. Option includes call and put option and other various combinations.

Call option

Call option means right to buy stock or index at particular strike price in predetermined time period. Option usually expire on third Friday of month. Stock could go up or down or stay the same. These are three direction stock can move. Only way you can make money with call option is that stock goes up more than strike price and premium you have paid for that option in predetermined period of time. You have only one out of three chance to make money.

To give you example Microsoft stock is trading at 90 dollars currently in May 2018. Based on information you have, you feel like stock is going to go up.You buy one call option (which control 100 shares) of Microsoft expiring on July 20th,2018 at 90 dollar strike price and you pay 5 dollars for it.

As we discussed Microsoft stock could go up, down or stay the same. If Microsoft goes down or stay the same or move up by less than 5 dollars, we lose money on call option. Only way we make money if Microsoft stock goes up by more than 5 dollars by July 20th,2018.So you see that options are stacked against us when we buy option and we could only make money only when stock moves 1 out of 3 ways it can move.

Put option

Put option when you have bearish prediction about stock and you think that stock will move down. To give you example that you think that Tesla stock is overpriced at 300 dollars and will go down.You buy 1 put option (controls 100 shares) expiring on July 20th,2018. You pay 10 dollars for this option. Tesla stock could go up, stay the same or move down. You have only one out of three chances you will make money. Only way you make money on this put option if Tesla stock goes down by more than 10 dollars by July 20th,2018.

So you see that odds are stacked against you since you do not know what future is going to bring for us.

With above in mind 80% of investor who buys option lose money.

You can also sell option which improves your odd slightly but if you have stock and you sell covered call option you lose upside potential of that stock. If you sell naked put option then you have tremendous downside risk with it. You better like that stock at the price you sold put on, otherwise if stock keep going down you may lose lot of money and you have to sell it at a loss after you were assigned that put option. Only way you could benefit by selling option on that stock is that you like the stock at this price and you were going to buy it otherwise. Now you can get stock at discounted price or paid put premium to you since stock stay above your strike price.

Overall options trading is very risky and 80% of investor lose money trading option. If you are busy doing your job or enjoying retirement I will not waste my time or money in trading option.

Chapter 6: Social Security

Social security

Here are some salient facts about social security program.

Social security is important part of retirement and could contribute half of money for your retirement needs.

Social security was started by president Roosevelt in 1935 and in 1972 congress approved annual cost of living increase for social security. In 1965 congress approved Medicare, a program of federal health insurance for people 65 year old or older.

You pay 6.2% of your wages for social security and 1.45% for Medicare (total 7.65% of wages) and your employer pays 7.65% of wages on your behalf for your social security and Medicare during your working years.

Most of current retiree will get full benefit at age 65-67 year, based on year they were born. Your spouse will also qualify for half of your benefit at her retirement even if she has not worked .She may also qualify for higher benefit at retirement age based on her wages during working years.

Your benefits are calculated based on your social security contribution made during your lifetime (Retirement benefit are based on 35 years of highest indexed earning).

If you take social security benefit early at age 62, you will lose your benefit in excess of 30% and I strongly advise against it unless you are in really poor health and your chances of long term survival are very low . You can get full social security benefit at age 65-67 year depending on year of your birth. You can increase your benefit by 8% per year , 32% for four years if you take social security benefit at age 70 . If you are in good health I will recommend taking social security at age 70 to have enhanced benefit for lifetime. Once you take social security your payment will increase based on cost of living increase on yearly basis.

Regarding future of social security if federal government does not do anything, than in future they have to reduce benefit to 75% or advance age at which you qualify for social security. I hope federal government make some changes to continue social security program at current level.

Chapter 7: Gold and Precious Metals

Gold and Precious Metals

Investing in gold or precious metal is not a good option for long term and price of gold is determined by fear, inflation or demand. Gold does not pay any interest or dividends. There is cost involved in gold storage. Gold does provide small hedge against inflation and there have been situation that countries have resorted to excessive printing of currency which have created significant inflation . As you may be aware of that US have come off from Gold standard during Nixon presidency.

If you like gold as inflation hedge, I will not put more than 5% of portfolio in Gold/Precious metal.

Chapter 8:   Commodity future and Currency trading

Investing in commodities future and currency trading is very risky and should be left to professional traders who have tremendous advantage over regular investors.

It is like gambling for individual investor and I will stay out of it.

Chapter 9: Asset Allocation

HOW TO PUT IT TOGATHER / ASSET ALLOCATION

In the end, your success is determined by getting the best possible return with taking least amount of risk with choices available. I also want to define two term " NEED money and WANT money".

NEED money is money you need to run household expenses in retirement which includes money for housing (mortgage payment including property taxes and property insurance and yearly property maintenance expenses), Utilities, Food, Clothing, Health insurance, Auto insurance,Telephone,Television etc.

WANT money is money you want to use for travel, addition to your house, expensive car, donation to family/needy and some extra toys like boat, motor cycles, expensive painting, outings etc.

Age 25-50

Put 80-100% of your money in stock market via ROTH IRA or 401 K at work.

You can buy Total World stock index fund (VTWSX) or ETF VT from Vanguard. This fund or ETF invest in over 8000 stocks all over globe and has expense ratio less than 0.1%. Since above fund predominantly invest in Large cap stocks, you can allocate 30% of stock portion in small cap index mutual fund or ETF like VB from Vanguard or I share ETF like IJR which have expense ratio less than 0.1%. If you are afraid of stock market fluctuation put 20% of money in Total Bond index fund with low expense ratio (VBTLX). This bond fund has over 8000 bond and has expense ratio of 0.05%.Vanguard has been leader of low cost index fund and will be good company to use for investing.

Age 50-65

Start adding money aggressively in your fixed income portfolio (Bonds/Real estate). If you are in higher than 22% federal tax bracket, use municipal bond / municipal bond fund with low expense ratio, if you are in less than 22% federal income tax bracket use total bond market index fund or ETF (BND) . Aim is to get so much capital in fixed income/real estate portfolio, so that at age 60-65, you are getting your need money from Bonds/ Real estate and it will be supplemented by social security at age 65-70 years

Age 65 onward

If you are within 5 years of retirement or already in retirement I will recommend first determine how much money you need for basic needs like food, shelter, clothing, health insurance etc. & day to day living.(NEED MONEY).

Suppose you need $4000 per month, $48000 per year, then approximately one third to one half money (33%--50%) is coming from social security depending on how much money you have contributed to social security in last 35 years. Remainder of money $24000—32000/ year need to come from bond/real estate investing. Using 4% return from bond market / real estate investing you need to have around 600,000--800000 dollars invested in bond market / real estate market depending on your expertise and preference (Investment return of around 4%) . Do not worry if you do not have capital to make that kind of return then you can invest directly in residential / commercial rental real estate to get 6-8% return but this may involve some work in term of managing properties directly without having to pay additional fee to Management Company. In addition social security income/ Dividends from stock market could supplement your fixed income need.(Need money).Qualified dividends from stock market is taxed at lower rate.

If you are in higher income bracket (> 22%), you could go for long term general obligation muni bond (AAA or AA rated) yielding 3-4% without worry about federal taxes & you could focus in your state muni bonds to avoid state income tax also.

If you are in low income tax bracket you could invest for basic income in index bond ETF or mutual fund / real estate or REITS for getting after tax return of 3.5-4%.

As far payment from social security I recommend taking social security at age of 70 to get most payment from federal government unless you are in poor health then you could start taking your social security at retirement age of 65 to 67 years.

I also recommend taking Medicare at age 65 & also buying supplemental insurance to cover outpatient visit & medicine both of which have substantial cost , without supplemental insurance.

Once you have decent income coming from fixed income investment including bonds, real estate and social security to fund day to day lifestyle. I recommend putting rest of money in broad based ETF / mutual fund with low expense ratio (70% of capital in VT or vanguard total stock world index mutual fund and 30% of stock allocation in small cap ETF like VB or IJR) to deal with cost of inflation and unforeseen need in future.

Once you are not dependent on stock market for your day to day need you will not worry about stock market fluctuations during your golden years in retirement.

Stock market investment is there for your WANT money (WANT MONEY is for pleasure trip, donations, luxury car and costly addition to your house and inflation need). Depending on your saving you could have as little as 25% of your portfolio or as much as 50% of your portfolio in stocks in retirement.

Since your need money is coming from bonds/real estate investment / social security, you don't have to worry or lose sleep over stock market fluctuation.

Chapter 10: Summary and Guidelines

SUMMARY / ROAD MAP   TO SECURE RETIREMENT

Age 5-25/30 years

1. **Focus on your education. If you are not interested in college education ,go to technical school or local college and learn skill which could feed you and your family and will be source of wealth for your lifetime.**

2. **Minimize debt by going to state university or local technical college and work part time.**

3. **Take time to choose your life partner because this could be most important decision of lifetime.**

AGE 25/30-65 years

1. **If you have dependents, Buy Term life insurance for 10-15 time your yearly expenses . Buy disability insurance pertaining to your skill and job and pay premium with after tax money so your benefit is not subject to taxation.**

2. Have emergency fund for 6-12 month expenses so in case you lose job, basic necessities are taken care off.

3. Pay your educational and other debt as fast as possible

4. Invest in company at least which your employer is matching and put up to $5500 / year in Roth IRA (preferably use stock fund to grow your money in accumulation phase of your life).

5. Accumulate 20% of money for down payment for house so you don't have to pay for private mortgage insurance, meanwhile rent apartment.

6. Start saving money for college education in 529 plan (Around 10-20 thousand total per child depending on their education potential.)

7. Buy house with 10-15 year fixed loan and make extra payments to pay loan as soon as possible.

Once your house is paid and children college education is taken care of around your age of 45-50 years

1. Focus on your retirement and put all your saving in retirement, at least 15% of your salary and increase Roth IRA to $7000 / year both for you and your spouse.

2. Asset allocation at this stage about 60% in stock market and around 40% in bonds/real estate market.

3. As age advances, increase your bond / real estate portfolio so your NEED money is coming from Bonds / Real estate investments and dividends from stock market.

AGE 65 year onward

1.   Design your portfolio so that your NEED money is coming from bonds / real estate / dividends from stock market supplemented by social security at age 70.

2.   Get Medicare at age 65 and buy supplemental insurance to cover for outpatient care and cost of medicines.

3. Once you have your NEED money coming from Bonds / Real estate / Social security put rest of your money in stock market (25-50% of portfolio) to deal with WANT money and inflation in future.

4. Enjoy your life without worry about day to day fluctuation in stock market.

These are guidelines to roadmap to security / wealth. Individual and family needs may vary and need help of a personal advisor to understand intricate needs of individual / family.

Thank You

I hope this short guide could be of service to you for future needs.